33d Congress, 2d Session. | HOUSE OF REPRESENTATIVES. | Ex. Doc. No. 47.

RAMSEY & CARMICK—CONTRACT.

LETTER

FROM

THE POSTMASTER GENERAL,

TRANSMITTING

Copy of a conditional mail contract; also copies of correspondence relative to the same.

February 1, 1855.—Referred to the Committee on the Post Office and Post Roads, and ordered to be printed.

Post Office Department,
Washington, January 31, 1855.

Sir: I have the honor to transmit herewith, in compliance with the resolution of the House of the 2d of January instant, a copy of the conditional contract made by my predecessor, Mr. Hubbard, with Messrs. Ramsey & Carmick, on the 3d of March, 1853, for the extension of two of the trips on the New Orleans and Vera Cruz line, from Vera Cruz, Mexico, via Acapulco, to San Francisco in California; also copies of all the correspondence relative to the same, and also relative to the change of schedule proposed on the line from New Orleans to Vera Cruz.

My views in regard to this contract were fully stated in my annual report to Congress of December 1, 1853, and are also contained in the correspondence herewith communicated. It was not deemed necessary to answer the letter of Robert G. Rankin, president of the Mexican Ocean Mail and Inland Company, dated November 23, 1853, and received at the department on the 30th of January, 1854. That they were not prepared to fulfil their conditional contract on the 23d of November, 1853, nine months after its execution, is therein conceded, and the department had neither the time nor desire to enter into a discussion of the irrelevant matters introduced into the body of that letter.

The objections which I entertained to the change of schedule on the New Orleans and Vera Cruz route, proposed, by Messrs. Harris & Morgan in their letter of the 26th October, 1853, were two-fold:

1st. That by authorizing the change proposed the original intent and object of my predecessor, Mr. Hubbard, in entering into the conditional contract with Messrs. Ramsey and Carmick—which was, to secure an additional semi-monthly mail between the Atlantic States and California by alternating at regular intervals with the present semi-monthly line via Panama—would have been entirely frustrated; and thus, instead of having a weekly mail between the Atlantic and Pacific, there would have been, as heretofore, only a semi-monthly communication.

2d. By changing the schedule so as to make connections at Acapulco with the steamers of the Pacific Mail Steamship Company, that company would receive not only their regular compensation under their contract with the government, but extra pay under the contract of Ramsey & Carmick, although no additional service was really rendered by them to the department or the public.

Authority having been given by Mr. Hubbard on the 7th of March, 1853, to the postmasters of New Orleans, San Diego, Monterey and San Francisco, to make up and send mails by the Vera Cruz and Acapulco line, containing such matter as was expressly directed to go by that line, I took the precaution to withhold from those officers the authority to send mails without first consulting the department, by instructing them, on the 23d of September following, to report to the department before delivering such mails, for further instructions, should the proprietors apply for them. My object in issuing those instructions was simply to enable the department to be fully satisfied that all mails forwarded by that route were committed to the care and custody of competent and proper persons, and would be safely transported through Mexico. It does not appear, however, that any application has ever been made by Messrs. Ramsey & Carmick for a mail to be conveyed by that route, as no report from any postmaster to that effect has been received at this department.

I have the honor to be, sir, very respectfully, your obedient servant,

JAMES CAMPBELL.

Hon. LINN BOYD,
Speaker of House of Representatives.

No. 9—$424,000 PER ANNUM.

This article of contract, made the fifteenth day of February, in the year one thousand eight hundred and fifty-three, between the United States (acting in this behalf by their Postmaster General) and Albert C. Ramsey and Edward H. Carmick, William H. Aspinwall and Edwin Bartlett, of the city of New York; Silas C. Herring, Elihu Townsend, Simeon Draper, and R. B. Coleman, of the same place, *witnesseth:* That whereas, by an act of Congress, passed March 3, 1845, entitled "An act to provide for the transportation of the mail between the United States and foreign countries, and for other purposes," the Postmaster General is authorized to contract for the transportation of the United States mail between any of the ports of the United

States and a port or ports of any foreign power whenever, in his opinion, the public interests will thereby be promoted; and whereas, by another act of Congress, passed March 3, 1851, entitled "An act to establish certain post-roads in the United States and the Territories thereof," the Postmaster General is authorized to enter into contracts, for a period not longer than four years, for transporting through any foreign country the mails of the United States, and that in making such contracts, the Postmaster General shall be bound to select the speediest, safest, and most economical route; and whereas notice has been given by advertising, in accordance with the directions of said act, for inviting proposals for mail contracts, under and by virtue of the acts aforesaid; and whereas Albert C. Ramsey and Edward H. Carmick have been accepted, according to law, as contractors for transporting the mail on route No. 9, from Vera Cruz, via Acapulco, to San Francisco and back, twice a month, according to the schedule hereinafter mentioned, in thirteen days each way, being an extension of two of the trips on the New Orleans and Vera Cruz line through Mexico, for the purpose of conveying the mail, and thus making one through-line in sixteen days between New Orleans and San Francisco, at and for the sum of four hundred and twenty-four thousand dollars per year, for and during the term commencing from the time Congress shall ratify this contract, and ending four years from that date, with the right reserved to the Postmaster General to continue it one year longer, at the same terms:

Now, therefore, the said Albert C. Ramsey and Edward H. Carmick, contractors, and Silas C. Herring, Elihu Townsend, Simeon Draper, Robert B. Coleman, William H. Aspinwall, and Edwin Bartlett, their sureties, do jointly and severally undertake, covenant, and agree with the United States, and do bind themselves:

1st. To carry said mail within the times fixed in the annexed schedule of departures and arrivals, and so carry until said schedule is altered by the authority of the Postmaster General of the United States, as hereinafter provided, and then to carry according to said altered schedule.

2d. To carry said mail in a safe and secure manner, free from wet or other injury, in weather-proof bags and vehicles on the land route, and in a separate and convenient apartment on shipboard, to be suitably fitted up under order of the department, at the expense of the contractors, for the assorting and safe-keeping of the mails, and for the sole and exclusive occupation, use, and accommodation of the Post Office Department and its mail-agent, if the Postmaster General shall require it for the use and accommodation of the mail and mail-agent, and such mail-agent is to be conveyed without further charge.

In case the contractors fail to furnish such suitable accommodations, the department shall have the right to provide the bags, vehicles, or apartments, or other suitable accommodations, at the expense of the contractors.

3d. To take the mail and every part of it from, and deliver it and every part of it into, the post office at San Francisco, and to and from the mail steamers at Vera Cruz on the New Orleans and Vera Cruz line, and also to deliver and receive the mails at San Diego and Mon terey, regularly by each trip going and returning, as is now done by the "Pacific Mail Steamship Company."

They also undertake, covenant, and agree with the United States, and do bind themselves, jointly and severally, as aforesaid, to be answerable for the person to whom the said contractors shall commit the care and transportation of the mail, and accountable to the United States for any damages which may be sustained by the United States through his unfaithfulness or want of care; and that the said contractors will discharge any carrier of said mail whenever required to do so by the Postmaster General; also, that they will not transmit by themselves or their agent, or be concerned in transmitting, commercial intelligence more rapidly than by mail, and they will not carry out of the mail letters or newspapers which should go by post; and that they will not, knowingly, convey any person carrying on the business of transporting letters or other mail matter without the consent of the department; and further, that the said contractors will convey, without additional charge, post-office blanks, mail bags, and the special agents of the department, on the exhibition of their credentials.

They further undertake, covenant, and agree with the United States, that the said contractors will collect quarterly, if required by the Postmaster General, of postmasters on said route, the balances due from them to the General Post Office, and faithfully render an account thereof to the Postmaster General in the settlement of quarterly accounts, and will pay over to the General Post Office all balances remaining in their hands.

For which services, when performed, the said Albert C. Ramsey and Edward H. Carmick, contractors, are to be paid by the said United States the sum of four hundred and twenty-four thousand dollars a year, to wit: quarterly, in the months of May, August, November, and February, through the postmasters on the route, or otherwise, at the option of the Postmaster General of the United States; said pay to be subject, however, to be reduced or discontinued by the Postmaster General, as hereinafter stipulated, or to be suspended in case of delinquency.

It is hereby stipulated and agreed by the said contractors and their sureties, that the Postmaster General may increase the service or change the schedule, he allowing a pro rata increase of compensation within the restrictions imposed by law for the additional service required; but the contractors may, in case of increased service or change of schedule, relinquish the contract, on timely notice, if they prefer it to the change.

It is hereby also stipulated and agreed by the said contractors and their sureties, that in all cases there is to be a forfeiture of the pay of a trip when the trip is not performed, and of not more than three times the pay of a trip when the trip is not duly performed and no sufficient excuse for the failure is furnished; a forfeiture of at least one-fourth part of it when the running is so far behind time as to lose connexion with a depending mail, unless it is shown that the same was not caused by neglect, or want of proper skill or misconduct, and a forfeiture of a due proportion of it when a grade of service is rendered inferior to the mode of conveyance above stipulated; and that these forfeitures may be increased into penalties of a higher amount, according to the nature or frequency of the failure, and the importance of the mail; also that fines may be imposed upon the contractors, unless the delinquency be satisfactorily explained to the Postmaster General in due time, for failing to take from or deliver at a post office, or a steam-vessel, the mail, or any part of it; for suffering it to be wet, injured, lost, or destroyed; for carrying it in a place or manner that exposes it to depredation, loss or injury, by being wet, or otherwise; for refusing, after demand, to carry a mail by any vessel or other vehicle which the contractors run or are concerned in running on the route beyond the number of trips above specified; or for not arriving at the time set in the schedule, unless not caused by neglect or want of proper skill, or by misconduct. And for setting up or running an express to transmit letters or commercial intelligence in advance of the mail, or for transporting knowingly, or after being informed, any one engaged in transporting letters or mail matter in violation of the laws of the United States, a penalty of five hundred dollars may be exacted for each offence, and for each article so carried.

And it is hereby further stipulated and agreed by the said contractors and their sureties that the Postmaster General may annul the contract for repeated failures; for violating the post office laws; for disobeying the instructions of the department; for refusing to discharge a carrier, or any other person having charge of the mail by his direction, when required by the department; for assigning the contract without the consent of the Postmaster General; for setting up or running an express as aforesaid, or for transporting persons, conveying mail matter out of the mail as aforesaid; or whenever the contractors or either of them shall become a postmaster, assistant postmaster, or member of Congress; and this contract shall in all its parts be subject to the terms and requisitions of an act of Congress passed on the twenty-first day of April, in the year of our Lord one thousand eight hundred and eight, entitled "An act concerning public contracts."

And it is hereby further stipulated and agreed by the said contractors, that the steam-vessels for the service between San Francisco and Acapulco shall be of a class contemplated by the act of Congress, passed March 3, 1845, entitled "An act to provide for the transportation of the mail between the United States and foreign countries, and for other purposes;" and that the same shall be delivered to the United States, or their proper officer, on demand made, for the purpose of being converted into vessels of war, according to the tenor and terms of the said act.

And it is hereby further expressly understood that this contract is to have no force or validity until it shall have received the sanction of the Congress of the United States, by the passage of an appropriation to carry it into effect.

In witness whereof, the said Postmaster General has caused the seal of the Post Office Department to be hereto affixed, and has attested the same by his signature; and the said contractors and their sureties have hereunto set their hands and seals the day and year set opposite their names, respectively.

S. D. HUBBARD, [SEAL.] March 3, 1853.
Postmaster General.
WM. H. ASPINWALL, [SEAL.] March 3, 1853.
EDWIN BARTLETT, [SEAL.] March 3, 1853.
By Wm. H. Davidge, their Att'y.
ALBERT C. RAMSEY. [SEAL.] February 25, 1853.
EDWARD H. CARMICK. [SEAL.] February 25, 1853.
SILAS C. HERRING. [SEAL.] February 25, 1853.
ELIHU TOWNSEND. [SEAL.] February 25, 1853.
SIMEON DRAPER. [SEAL.] February 25, 4853.
R. B. COLEMAN. [SEAL.] February 25, 1853.
THE MEXICAN OCEAN MAIL AND INLAND COMPANY, [SEAL.] February 25, 1853.
By Robert G. Rankin, President.

Signed, sealed, and delivered by the Postmaster General in the presence of—
JAMES LAWRENSON.
R. T. MCLAIN.

And by the other parties hereto in the presence of—
J. B. NOTT, witness for A. C. Ramsey, S. Draper, and R. B. Coleman, and Edward H. Carmick.
EDWARD S. GOULD, witness to S. C. Herring.

Witness to Wm. H. Davidge's signature, as attorney of Wm. H. Aspinwall and Edwin Bartlett—
JAMES LAWRENSON.
R. T. MCLAIN.

Witness to R. G. Rankin's signature—
JNO. T. HOWARD.

—

I hereby certify that I am well acquainted with Albert C. Ramsey, and Edward H. Carmick, and Silas C. Herring, Elihu Townsend, Simeon Draper, and R. B. Coleman, and the condition of their property; and that, after full investigation and inquiry, I am well satisfied that they are good and sufficient sureties for the amount in the foregoing contract.

WM. V. BRADY,
Postmaster at New York.

The schedule of Departures and Arrivals.

Leave Vera Cruz on the 4th and 17th of each month. Arrive at Acapulco by the 9th and 22d of each month.

Leave Acapulco on the 9th and 22d of each month. Arrive at San Francisco by the 17th and 30th of each month.

Leave San Francisco on the 8th and 24th of each month. Arrive at Acapulco by the 16th and 1st of each month.

Leave Acapulco on the 16th and 1st of each month. Arrive at Vera Cruz by the 21st and 6th of each month.

POST OFFICE DEPARTMENT,
March 7, 1853.

GENTLEMEN: The postmasters of New Orleans, San Francisco, Monterey and San Diego, will be authorized to send a mail by the Vera Cruz and Acapulco line, containing letters or papers expressly directed to go by that line, when said communication is open, and you are prepared to carry a mail, with the express understanding that neither this department nor the government is to be in any way holden for any expenses attending such service; but, as provided in the contract, it is left for Congress to determine whether the contract is to be sanctioned by an appropriation to carry it into effect—the pay, if any, for said service commencing only in accordance with the terms of the contract made February 15, 1853.

I am, respectfully, your obedient servant,
S. D. HUBBARD,
Postmaster General.

Messrs. RAMSEY & CARMICK, *New York.*

POST OFFICE DEPARTMENT,
March 7, 1853.

SIR: You are hereby authorized to make up and send a mail by the Vera Cruz and Acapulco line, containing letters or papers expressly directed to go by that line, when said communication is open, and the contractors are prepared to carry a mail on the terms of their contract of February 15, 1853. You would do well, perhaps, to advertise to the above effect, adding that all letters, &c., not marked as above indicated, will be forwarded by the Panama route.

Respectfully, your obedient servant,
S. D. HUBBARD,
Postmaster General.

POSTMASTER,
San Francisco, California.

[Same to postmasters of New Orleans, San Diego, and Monterey.]

OFFICE OF THE MEXICAN OCEAN MAIL AND INLAND CO.,
New York, June 15, 1853.

MY DEAR SIR: The position that our company sustains to the government, (as the real parties by contract,) to execute the mail contracts with Messrs. Ramsey & Carmick, renders it proper that the Post Office Department should be advised of the state of forwardness on the part of the contractors to fulfil the contracts.

Our vice president, Colonel Albert C. Ramsey, is now in Mexico assigning the stations. In all this month and next month, the coaches, wagons, and literas will be in Mexico—portions of them being on their way now. By August 10 the mules and horses (1,000) will be down from Coahuila, and we then expect to make the regular transit across.

Although the contracts only require a bi-monthly mail, we are making all our arrangements for a *daily line* of transit across Mexico, feeling justified by the assurances we have from Mexico. We shall also establish a weekly line of steamers from New Orleans to Vera Cruz, (one steamer is now running there, and another now building;) and with the use of the new *envelopes*, (when they appear,) we shall actually afford a weekly line from New Orleans to San Francisco; and if the steamers on the Pacific could be arranged, we could make a daily line to San Francisco in sixteen days. Our land route will be daily, in any case, on account of our Mexican facilities.

We have purchased and ordered the whole of the rolling stock for the transit, and parties are now in Mexico clearing obstructions, and we shall not, I think, require the full time allowed by the contract for the transit, although trial only will verify our expectations.

We already have a margin in our favor in the gulf service, as our steamer, the "Texas," has performed the duty in sixty hours; and the Pacific service has been done in twenty-four and thirty hours less than schedule time. Our recent reports from Mexico justify us in the expectation of carrying the mails in fourteen days from New Orleans to San Francisco, and six months of experimental operation will, I think, show the feasibility of doing the regular service in within fifteen days.

In conclusion, I would add that we are exerting every energy in pushing the thing up, and shall spare neither time nor money in proving the truthfulness of all our positions.

An estafette mail will be carried from Vera Cruz and New Orleans to San Francisco next month, until the service becomes regular.

I am, with great respect, your obedient servant,

ROBT. G. RANKIN,
President.

We have the *highest* assurance of *our* favorable position in Mexico.

Hon. JAMES CAMPBELL,
Postmaster General U. S., &c.

POST OFFICE DEPARTMENT, *July* 9, 1853.

SIR: Your letter of the 15th ultimo came duly to hand. My attention having been specially called to the circumstances connected with the contemplated line to the Pacific via Vera Cruz and Acapulco, I feel it my duty, after due deliberation, to inform you that the conditional contract entered into between my predecessor, Mr. Hubbard, and Messrs. Ramsey and Carmick, for the conveyance of the mails over this line to San Francisco, does not meet with my approbation.

In the first place, as at present advised, I consider the route impracticable for mail purposes.

In the second place, the sums of money yearly drawn from the treasury for contracts, which have for several years been, and are still in force, for the transportation of the mails between the Atlantic and the Pacific, are very considerable, amounting to about $731,868. In view of this fact, and of the many sections and neighborhoods, in the different States, which are either greatly restricted in, or deprived altogether of mail facilities, it appears to me both inexpedient and unjust to go into the expenditure of a still further sum of $424,000 for the service in question.

Moreover, I disapprove of the principle upon which this contract is made. In my opinion, if the Postmaster General has the right to make such a contract at all, it ought to be made without the restriction or limitation contained in yours, by which its force or validity is made to depend upon the passage of an appropriation by Congress to carry it into effect. I am unwilling to recognise any contingency of this kind, because, although the contractors may, under such conditional arrangement, establish no legal claim for compensation, they may, nevertheless, go on and incur expenses, in the expectation that they will be paid, and Congress, more from private sympathy than from public policy or right, be at length induced to yield to a measure to which its prior sanction never could have been obtained.

I am, respectfully, your obedient servant,

JAMES CAMPBELL,
Postmaster General.

Robt. G. Rankin, Esq.,
Pres't of the Mexican Ocean Mail and Inland Co., N. Y.

Post Office Department, *September* 23, 1853.

Sir: Should the proprietors of the Vera Cruz, Acapulco, and San Francisco line apply for mail to take over their route, under the conditional order of the late Postmaster General, dated 7th March, 1853, before delivering such mail to them, you will report to department for further instructions.

Very respectfully, your obedient servant,

JAMES CAMPBELL,
Postmaster General.

Postmaster,
New Orleans, Louisiana.

To Postmaster at San Diego, California: Same.

J. C.

To Postmaster at Monterey, California: Same.

J. C.

To Thos. J. Henley, Esq., San Francisco, California: Same.

J. C.

WASHINGTON, *October* 26, 1853.

DEAR SIR: The Mexican Ocean Mail and Inland Company, and Charles Morgan, of New York, (through the agency of the undersigned,) present the following facts, and ask such decision as an impartial consideration of this memorial may produce. The company (having obtained from the government of Mexico peculiar and well-authenticated privileges, whereby they were enabled to present to the United States Post Office Department a schedule of mail service which should insure the transmission of mails between New Orleans and San Francisco in the short space of sixteen days) urged the department for a mail contract authorizing the service, which was granted, subject to an appropriation by Congress for payment. Thereupon the company commenced proceedings for putting the route into active operation. Proper agents were despatched to Mexico, and have been actively engaged in overcoming such obstacles as, unremoved, would have impeded rapid transit across that country. Roads were improved, others made; coaches, harness, mules, and horses have been purchased, and a large portion of them are already on the route, ready to commence the carrying of the mails. In connexion with, and forming a portion of, this through-route, a mail service from New Orleans to Vera Cruz has been put into operation, the schedule for which was so arranged as to meet at Acapulco with the mail steamers on the Pacific, insuring a proper connexion on that end of the line. Thus nothing stood in the way of the successful operation of the route, save the obstacles on the land, which, being overcome, would enable us at once to perform our contract in the specified time; but now that arrangements are completed for this portion on the service, your memorialists find that an alteration in the running on the Pacific has thrown out of gear this well-arranged system. By the present schedule between New Orleans and Vera Cruz, it is impossible to meet the Pacific steamers, as they now run, at Acapulco, without suffering long delays at the latter point, entirely ruining the efficacy of this otherwise desirable medium of transit. The undersigned, C. Morgan, now urges that a knowledge of the existence of a through-service to San Francisco was the inducement for his accepting the portion of service between New Orleans and Vera Cruz; as, upon the successful working of the through-route, he depended for any profits that might inure to his ships from his connexion therewith. He has already put upon the route a first-class steamship of over 1,100 tons burden, and is building another of about 1,500 tons burden for the same purpose; which two vessels will embrace an investment of nearly $300,000 for this first portion of the enterprise. The company depend upon appropriations by Congress for the means of remuneration; and as such appropriations can only be secured by proofs of the practicability of the through-route, as per schedule, they, together, ask your consideration of the efforts they have made, and the moneys they have expended, under inducements the Post Office Department held out to them, for such efforts and expenditures, *by granting a through-service and arranging schedule for connexion;* and respectfully petition that you will so alter the schedule between New Orleans and Vera Cruz for the two trips per month, now being performed, as will give them an opportunity of proving to Congress that this is by far the most expeditious route yet opened to the rich commerce of California; which proofs, they feel, must necessarily insure the appropriations that shall furnish the means to enable them eventually to carry the mails between the two great points in the short space of thirteen days! Believing that your sense of justice, and desire for advancing the mails in accordance with the progressive ideas of this essentially progressive age, will induce an assent to their prayer, they have the honor herewith to submit such *temporary* schedule, for the said two trips per month, as shall furnish the desired proofs; and, with sentiments of regard and esteem, subscribe, respectfully, yours,

The MEXICAN OCEAN MAIL AND INLAND CO.;
and CHARLES MORGAN,
per Harris & Morgan, *of New Orleans.*

Hon. James Campbell,
Postmaster General United States.

Schedule.

Leave New Orleans 7th and 22d;
Arrive at Vera Cruz 10th and 25th.
Leave Vera Cruz 14th and 29th;
Arrive at New Orleans 17th and 2d.

Office of the Mexican Ocean Mail and Inland Co.,
New York, October 29, 1853.

Dear Sir: Herewith please find a letter addressed to our firm from the president of the Pacific Mail Steamship Company, explaining why the schedule of running on the Pacific has been changed, (thus rendering *useless* the *present schedule* between New Orleans and Vera Cruz;) and, further, approving the schedule which we had the honor of submitting for your consideration in our memorial, dated in Washington, D. C. Trusting the views of our case, to which your attention has been called, will induce a favorable decision, we have the honor to subscribe, with sentiments of regard and respect,

Your obedient servants,
HARRIS & MORGAN.

Hon. James Campbell,
Postmaster General United States.

[For the Commercial Advertiser.]

Office of the Mexican Ocean Mail and Inland Co.,
New York, October 27, 1853.

In your issue of Wednesday evening, in the postscript of telegraphic news from Mexico, an important error occurred in relation to the transmission of San Francisco news by our route. Your correspondent says: "The news came over the New Mexico or Ramsey route, and occupied about twenty-four days in its transmission." The facts are as follows: The news left San Francisco on the 1st of October by the Nicaragua steamer Pacific; it arrived at Acapulco on the 8th, crossed Mexico, and arrived at Vera Cruz on the 12th, where the news remained from the 12th until the 22d, the regular sailing day of the Texas, (the steamer that carried the news, instead of the Mexico, as stated in your article.) If our steamer had left Vera Cruz on the arrival of the news from Acapulco, our merchants would have had the market prices in fifteen days from San Francisco via New Orleans. If it should be asked why the Texas did not sail until the 22d, the only reply we have to offer is, that she was running on schedule time appointed by the Post Office Department, and until that schedule is altered the delay is likely to recur. With a proper connexion, our line can deliver mails from San Francisco, into New Orleans weekly, in less than sixteen days.

Respectfully, your obedient servant,

ROBERT G. RANKIN, *President.*

Be pleased to observe, by extract from Commercial Advertiser, the transmission of California news from California, by our route, in fourteen days!

H. & M.

PACIFIC MAIL STEAMSHIP COMPANY,
New York, October 28, 1853.

GENTLEMEN: Having examined carefully the schedule proposed by you for running on the route between New Orleans and Vera Cruz, so as to connect at Acapulco with our steamers between Panama and San Francisco, I beg leave to inform you that it meets our approval.

When our company commenced to run weekly boats, the schedule of the Texas was arranged to conform to the movements of those extra boats. It happened, however, that the United States Mail Steamship Company, although willing to perform extra service, and to let that service speak for itself to Congress, was not willing to bind itself as the government required, so as to shut out all prospect of extra remuneration by a liberal legislature for extra duty; and, consequently, the steamers, on intermediate weeks, on this side, were withdrawn. The connexion being thus cut off, our company was obliged to discontinue its weekly trips, after the schedule of the Vera Cruz and Acapulco route had been arranged to conform to those trips.

My understanding with Mr. Rankin is, that when the route is fairly opened, we will run steamers in the Pacific in due connexion; and I am prepared to assign this duty to two of our smaller first-class steamers the moment I am justified in so doing. Until then, the merits of the route can be tested by arranging a schedule to conform to the arrivals at Acapulco, and, as far as possible, to the departures thence for San Francisco of our steamers now running; and the interests of the government and of the public unite in recommending such a course.

Very truly, yours,

WM. H. ASPINWALL, *President.*

Messrs. HARRIS & MORGAN.

POST OFFICE DEPARTMENT,
November 3, 1853.

GENTLEMEN: In answer to your letter of the 26th ultimo, I have to state that, at the request of Mr. Carmick, the contractor, the present schedule of the New Orleans and Vera Cruz route was arranged to connect with the contemplated route across from Vera Cruz to Acapulco, which it was proposed to run in due connexion with an independent line of steamers between Acapulco and San Francisco—thus, with the route via Panama, giving a mail four times, instead of twice a month, between the Atlantic States and California. It was not the intention to connect at Acapulco with the steamers of the Panama line, but, as above remarked, to establish an additional semi-monthly mail to run, via Vera Cruz and Acapulco, alternately at regular intervals with the line via Panama.

This arrangement was made with my predecessor, Mr. Hubbard, with whom, as Postmaster General, also a conditional contract was entered into for the part of the service between Vera Cruz and San Francisco, which contract was to take effect *only from the time it should be ratified by Congress;* nor was it to have any force or validity whatever until it should receive the sanction of Congress by the passage of an appropriation to carry it into effect. No such sanction has as yet been given by Congress; but, apart from this, and without troubling you with my views on the whole subject, it is simply necessary for me to say that there can be no recognition by this department of any arrangement by which the additional semi-monthly mail, clearly contemplated by the then Postmaster General, can be dispensed with.

The application, therefore, for a change of schedule on the route from New Orleans to Vera Cruz, must now be considered without reference to any trips it may be proposed to run in connexion therewith beyond. The contract requires three trips a month; you propose but two, and it is unnecessary for me to say that the number of trips stipulated for in the contract will be required.

I am, very respectfully, your obedient servant,

JAMES CAMPBELL.

Messrs. HARRIS & MORGAN,
New Orleans, La.

WASHINGTON, *November* 12, 1853.

DEAR SIR: It is with great reluctance that I encroach upon your time at this particular season of your official duties; but what I have to say can be read at your leisure, without much inconvenience.

After my interview with you, yesterday, I was impressed with the idea that you had received from some quarter erroneous and unfavorable views in regard to this great national enterprise that I am so deeply interested in. I trust, however, that you will not permit any such influence to operate in your mind without affording us an opportunity to be heard. I consider it a duty I owe you and your high position to explain, in a frank and upright way, the true object we have in view in regard to this project; it is to test the merits of this route for a mail communication, the benefit of which will accrue to the country, the government, and those engaged in perfecting it. We have asked no remuneration from the government while pursuing this enterprise, but have gone to work, at our own expense, and proved the entire feasibility of this rapid communication, without the least hope or expectation that the department should in any way be subjected, either directly or indirectly, to an acknowledgment of responsibility for future remuneration. We desire to establish a great national highway from ocean to ocean, over a route in which there is a saving of 1,800 miles, between New Orleans and San Francisco; and the day is not far distant when all the present routes will only be secondary to it. This opinion is based on reasonable grounds: first, the saving of time; and, second, the beauty of the country, and the salubrious climate over which the route passes. There is but one opinion on this subject among all Californians. We have conceived that, in offering to our government the facilities of a rapid mail communication on so important a route, we have a right to expect from that government a liberal encouragement, at least by an expression favorable to an enterprise where so much energy and capital is invested. Our project has been fully investigated by the late cabinet, and, after their mature consideration, it was acted upon. The contract was sustained by an appeal of one-half of the United States Senate in a memorial to the department, and by the personal solicitation of the representatives from the South and West; also, by a memorial from the most influential citizens of Louisiana—the same being now on file in the department. General Rusk, who framed the law under which the contract was made, also urged the advantages of this communication on the department; among others were Senators Gwin and Soulé. This communication must depend entirely on its merits, and by its advantages for the public welfare. If it cannot offer greater inducements to the government than the present routes, it cannot expect to succeed; but if it can be proved that this is the speediest route, the law seems not to be violated while offering facilities on the part of the government to test so important an object. We have, however, proved beyond a doubt that the transit can be made from sea to sea in from three to four days, and I hope you may offer us your liberal co-operation, without involving in the least a compromise of the public interest; it is no more than we have a right to expect from the department. Governor Marcy, without looking into details, has expressed to me similar views, and says that our communication seems to hold out great national advantages, and he did not doubt but that you would look on it in a proper light. I feel confident that Congress will support any measure that can be proved of public utility for the South and West; and this is a southwestern measure, without any demands from the public treasury, to build steam-ships or railroads. I know the feeling that existed last Congress on this subject, and I feel confident that it will be supported by the South and West.

I have spent several years of intense labor and a large amount of money in bringing this enterprise to its present position. I have passed through many deep and almost impenetrable barriers, and no impediment shall stop the consummation of this great national work, save that of the hand of Providence. I am sustained by capital and energy, and I know no fail where perseverance can do the work. My future reputation and welfare is largely involved in the success of this project, and I sincerely beg that you will form no premature opinion on this subject against my interest. I do not, however, believe that you would do so, without an honest conviction of your judgment; but I do know that all enterprises must expect opposition from various causes. Envy is no small feature to contend with; and we have had to combat against it, solely upon the ground that we have not been disposed to divide our interest with others. The late administration was made aware of these facts, and they received with great caution any information coming from doubtful sources.

I most respectfully ask that you will give an order, permitting me, as one of the contractors, to carry a mail over this route from California, leaving it optional with persons to send by this way, and to designate the same on the letter; and in giving such an order, I wish you particularly to state that the department will in *no way be bound for any future remuneration for the service.*

Very respectfully, your obedient servant,

E. H. CARMICK.

Hon. JAMES CAMPBELL.

OFFICE OF THE MEXICAN OCEAN MAIL AND INLAND CO.,
November 23, 1853.

SIR: In accordance with a request from Messrs. Ramsey and Carmick, the contractors named in the contract hereinafter mentioned, I have the honor of reporting to your department *the real character of the relations this company sustains to the contract; the obstacles to the non-fulfilment of it by a date as early as was anticipated*; *and a few remarks explanatory of the route.*

On the 15th day of February, 1853, a contract was made by the United States government, acting by the Postmaster General, with Albert C. Ramsey and Edward H. Carmick, of Pennsylvania, to carry the United States mails between San Francisco and Vera Cruz, at certain definite and specific periods mentioned in the schedule of the contract, for the sum of $424,000 per year, for the period of four years, with the privilege of extending it one year if the Post Office Department thought proper. This contract was not of that liberal form heretofore characteristic of all the other ocean mail contracts, but was in a form of that specific and detailed character peculiar to any short land service, where time might be insured to a minute. The contract was, in fact, so stringent as to be incompatible with any but an honest intention to fulfil its spirit and letter, in which spirit it was, in fact, assumed by the parties associated in its performance. This contract was printed and sent to the Senate at its last session, and is now on its files. By the 5th section of the law of 1848 it is illegal for contractors to assign their contracts; and although aware that the department is not bound to recognise any but the contractors, yet, frankness enforces the propriety of saying that, by specific covenants, this company have agreed with Messrs. Ramsey and Carmick to fulfil all the conditions of the contract on their part, to be kept and performed in relation to the land service between Vera Cruz and Acapulco, and that similar covenants have been made with the Pacific Mail Steamship Company (William H. Aspinwall, esq., president) for the sea service between Acapulco and San Francisco. The contract distinctly specified that its schedule time (and in fact the spirit of the contract) was to the intent that it should form part and parcel of the contract for the gulf service, being an extension of two of the trips between New Orleans and Vera Cruz, made (under a specific law, August 30, 1852) with Mr. Carmick, so as to form, in its own language, *"one through-line in sixteen days between New Orleans and San Francisco."* The gulf contract is without any condition as to an appropriation; but the larger or Pacific contract is made contingent upon an appropriation by Congress for its approval. The question might be gravely raised, in looking at one contract as an integral part of the other, whether the appropriation by Congress of $70,000 (a trifle more than it was bid for and taken by Mr. Carmick, viz: $69,750) for the gulf service, was not an approval in terms of the Pacific contract, and discharged the condition of approval contained in it. But inasmuch as the parties associated in the enterprise have no covert policy to pursue, and have not yet been able to carry the mails in contract schedule time between Acapulco and San Francisco, (although they have carried it repeatedly in six days, or two days less than schedule time, between New Orleans and Acapulco,) they have no disposition to raise issues or ask for unearned appropriations. They presented their claims to the last administration on the sole integrity, feasibility, and celerity of their route; the proposals for the service were regularly advertised, and the contract awarded to the parties as the lowest bidders, but not until the most critical, searching, and minute examination was made of the practicability of the whole route. The investigation was pursued by the late Postmaster General Hubbard with a critical acumen that must have detected any imperfection. The grants made to this company by the Mexican government, and authenticated according to the highest forms known to the Mexican laws, were not only critically examined, but verified at Washington by the Mexican legation. These grants, instead of interfering with treaty stipulations, will, if honestly developed, prove most conservative elements in sustaining such stipulations by the promotion of commercial, social, and domestic intercourse, and by the infusion of fraternal comity in political and civil relations.

The obstacles to the non-fulfilment of the Pacific service.—As before stated, the contractors, this company, and the Pacific Mail Steamship Company, entered into mutual covenants, by which the latter company obligated themselves to carry the mails between San Francisco and Acapulco according to the contract and schedule time as therein set forth by the department. At the date of the contract the Pacific Mail Steamship Company were running a weekly line of steamers between Panama and San Francisco, in the weeks intervening with their semi-monthly mail; and the late administration intended, by this weekly line and the Vera Cruz and Acapulco route, to send a weekly instead of semi-monthly mail to San Francisco, and in sixteen days from New Orleans instead of twenty-eight days (the average at that time of the semi-monthly mails) from New York. The Pacific Mail Steamship Company withdrew their weekly line, which of course prevented the execution of the Pacific service in contract time until steamers could be placed on the line between Acapulco and San Francisco, and which this company are making arrangements to effect, not only in reference to the line from New Orleans, but from New York, so as to carry passengers in sixteen or eighteen days from New York to San Francisco. In consequence, however, of the (early) non-performance of the Pacific service in schedule time, it is understood that your department rescinded the order made by the late Postmaster General Hubbard for the postmasters at New Orleans, San Francisco, San Diego, Monterey, and to forward letters by this route. The disappointment of the contractors by the withdrawal of the weekly line was great and embarrassing, and disordered the whole arrangements of this company; and while we respectfully defer to the abstract correctness of the position taken by the Post Office Department on account of it, we yet hope that a great enterprise, so eminently calculated to benefit our commerce, and one so earnestly demanded by our southern and western citizens, as intimately connected with their interests, might have a little further time to place itself right before Congress and the department.

It is respectfully suggested, in this connexion, that the Gulf service is punctually performed twice a month, and will be three times a month as soon as the steamer "Vera Cruz," now nearly ready, can be finished; that the land-service, *as will be hereafter shown*, (see appendix,) has been performed, carrying an independent mail in sixty hours, (instead of one hundred and twenty hours, schedule time;) that this company have not asked for any special favors from the department—no advance on the appropriations—as other ocean mail companies have done; that no pay is asked for until the service is performed, and the money honestly and equitably earned; and that the 2d section of the law of March 3, 1851, is applicable to our case, viz: that the Postmaster General by this law "*shall be bound to select the speediest, safest, and most economical route.*"

We deprecate a negation of the contract by the department until further time is allowed us; and it is believed, in view of these facts and the spirit of the law last referred to, that our enterprise may receive an impartial consideration and presentation in your annual report on the Post Office Department. An official condemnation, emanating from the department under your administration, would be a serious obstacle in the development of the Mexican grants. *It is believed by many that the department had full power under the law to make the contract without the intervention of Congress for its approval;* but having been made with that contingency, it is now only asked that this enterprise may go before Congress on its own merits and integrity. A spirit of frank and honorable dealing renders it necessary for the undersigned to say, that a difference exists among the associated parties as to the real value and bearing of a government contract on this enterprise, and this difference may have reached the ears of the department.

Some of the parties believe that a government contract nationalizes the route, and gives it an importance superior to mere individual enterprise, and that the imperative necessity of *"making time"* insures more despatch. Others of the parties believe that a line of fast steamers from New Orleans to Vera Cruz, for the increasing southern and western travel from the valleys of the Mississippi and Ohio rivers, (composing the source of nearly seven-tenths of the whole resident population of California out of the city of San Francisco,) and another fast line of steamers from New York to Vera Cruz in six or seven days, by steamers built expressly for mail and passenger service, (and not naval service,) of about one thousand tons, in connexion with similar steamers from Acapulco to San Francisco in six days, would form a line that would take precedence of all others for celerity and certainty. Experience has exploded the idea that the mail and naval service can be performed by the same steamers; and an examination of the steamers now in the employ of the United States and mail-service department verifies the position that steamers suitable for a marine battery are too slow for "mail-service," and that the light and fast steamer which can be propelled three hundred and fifty miles in twenty-four hours is not suitable for a battery corresponding with her tonnage or power adequate to such speed. They believe that such a line, by this overland route, in sixteen, or eighteen, or twenty days, with an independent mail, would seriously diminish the postage receipts of the government, if not virtually supersede them, and render the present mail contracts a sinecure in the hands of the parties holding them. If offices should be opened in proper places for the receipt of mail-matter by advertisements, and the company should enclose that mail-matter in government-stamped envelopes, and guaranty the delivery of the mail by this route in six, eight, or ten days earlier than by the present government route, it is evident that the great bulk of the mail-matter would go by the quickest route, even at double, triple, or perhaps quadruple the present charge for postage. Such an independent mail (*clearly within the law*) would, it is confidently believed, measurably supersede the government mail, and reduce the postage to a pittance. Moreover, such an independent line, not being trammeled by government time, might connect with it English, West India, Australian, and Asiatic mails, all of which are specifically allowed by the several Mexican grants held by this company; and it is believed that the time is not far distant when an English express independent mail in forty-seven days, with Australia, will be in operation. It is also thought by some, that this company should be entirely disembarrassed in order to give an exclusive right to certain foreign interests.

Having frankly stated the difference of opinion on this subject among the associates in this enterprise, it is proper to say that a route nationalized by a public contract is the true official expression of the company's opinion, and the one which is now before the department. In conclusion on this point, it is respectfully suggested that this route is to be one of the great inter-oceanic routes of Atlantic, California, and Asiatic travel; that this enterprise may be fully developed by the present administration of our government without expense in its initial operations, but mainly by a prudent forbearance and official approbation, and by an order to carry such mail matter as our citizens may choose to send by it.

The enterprise is emphatically a southern and western one; although originated by Pennsylvanians, yet its vitality is due to New Orleans and southern influence, as the very numerous memorials on the files of the department or Congress, and signed by southern and western senators and members, will attest. The steamer Texas, which has been performing the Gulf service during the last summer, has carried a large amount of specie into New Orleans, (at the rate of one million and a quarter per annum;) and soon as the specie and express wagons of this company are fully at work, millions of dollars will flow into the New Orleans mint from the gold placers and silver mines of Mexico now being worked by American and Mexican combined skill.

Of the practicability of the route.—The direct mail route runs from Vera Cruz, by the way of Orizava, Cordova, Puebla, Matamoras, Chietla, Mitapec, Kalcozotitlan, Chilapa, Tixtla, to Acapulco, with branches from Puebla up to Mexico and via Cuernavaca.

This road was called by Humboldt the "*Asiatic road,*" as indicative of the maritime commerce of Spain; *and is the oldest road on the continent of America.* This route is no new thing, as many suppose, but the whole enterprise is but a recast of one developed long before our country had its name or a place among the nations of the earth.

Hundreds of millions of dollars have been received by the government of Old Spain, transported over this road, in the interchange of productions between the flotas of Spain and the galleons of the Indies, and millions of American commerce are yet to be rolled over it in the progress of American enterprise. The distance direct (as will be seen by the annexed itinerary) from Vera Cruz to Acapulco is 404 miles, and via the city of Mexico 517. Colonel Ramsey has since shortened this distance to under 390 miles, and it will be reduced to less than 350.

Over this road the materials and machinery for the vast coffee and sugar plantations of Mexico have to be transported, and these plantations for magnitude and productions are almost unequalled.

From the fact that the current of foreign travel has been turned towards the capital of Mexico, by the way of Jalapa and Perote, and also from the further fact that the very *limited amount of American* knowledge of Mexico is associated with the line of operations of the American army during the late war, less is publicly or *correctly* known of our lower, or more southern route, than of the upper or northern route. The lower and shorter route presents the facilities of being six hours shorter to Puebla, and of having lower grades, and a climate unequalled for healthfulness, salubrity, and intertropical luxuriance of productions.

There are features about the roads of Mexico generally that distinguish them from our northern roads; they are not muddy, having no frosts to produce periodic deterioration; they are only slightly disturbed during the rainy months of June, July, and August. The rains during these rainy months are not continuous, all-day rains, but fall in showers seldom longer than an hour, generally in the afternoons and at night, and the intervals between these showers are unclouded and salubrious. The whole geological formation of Mexico is eccentric, and the soil generally composed of the debris of matter of volcanic origin. Such materials form the best roads, and with an exemption from frosts, dust, mud, and rain, except in the rainy seasons, and with no fences to obstruct the facilities for turnpike, road-making, and travelling, presented in this part of Mexico, are unequalled.

It should be remembered that this company are not encumbered with the necessity of enormous expenditures for making canals, building railroads and plank-roads, to develop their resources; they have only to expend under $50,000 to make one of the finest roads in the finest climate of North America, to travel smoothly and pleasantly, at the rate of seven and ten miles per hour, from the Atlantic to the Pacific ocean.

From the certificate of Mr. Blumenkron, (see Appendix A,) a gentleman intimately acquainted with the whole route from personal observation, it will be seen that the facilities for the transportation of mails and passengers across the republic is the work of but little effort and expense; and from the extracts of Colonel Ramsey's letter, (see Appendix B,) it will be seen what has actually been done. From these statements—and they are daily corroborated by Americans and Mexicans who have passed over the route—it appears that the mails have been carried over (at the worst of all seasons, the rainy ones) in 50, 60, 70, 80, and 81 hours; that the letter of Mr. Tyler announces their arrival at Acapulco in six days from New Orleans, and that the mail time across may be reduced to 48 hours, and passenger time to 54.

The difficulties, dangers, and expense of mail transportation over this route are not comparable with the Panama route, as it formerly was, or even as it now is, as to the 17 miles yet uncovered by railroad; and this company confidently believe that they will be able to carry the mails over this route for a sum 50 per cent. per mile less than by the Panama route, and in a time under three days.

The company have placed a portion of their rolling stock upon the road, at present equal to the transportation of fifty passengers per week from ocean to ocean. This rolling stock consists of the very best built Albany and Troy post-coaches, Concord (New Hampshire) passenger, baggage, express and specie wagons, and about 500 horses and mules, (at the last report 493.)

It is hoped the next advices from Colonel Ramsey will give information that this rolling stock is in operation. It is intended to increase the rolling stock with the increase of travel. The local travel and business in Mexico will alone pay a large interest on the investment; and were there no connexion with steamers on either side, and as a mere stage route, the profits will be large, especially when that portion of the route through the State of Guerrero is properly worked and widened, and over a portion of the route the company hold the exclusive right of passage, ferries, tolls, &c., for fifty years.

This company apprehend no difficulty in transporting any mails on account of the weight, inasmuch as the company will be prepared to transport the English mails, between England and Australia, in under 47 days; and those mails, it is said, weigh 11 and 12 tons.

The remarkable feature in this route is, that it passes through a constant succession of cities, villages, ranches, &c., (few scarce ten miles apart,) and through a population as dense as might have been found on the old turnpike mail road from Albany to Buffalo before the age of railroads, or on any of the great leading mail routes of New York and Pennsylvania of a ratable distance; and the annexed itinerary, taken from official Mexican documents, verifies the position.

Fears have been expressed that robberies might endanger the mail, passengers, or property. This difficulty has been wondrously magnified, and is provided against, as the vehicles of this company are all armed with blunderbusses and revolvers; and small, but strong, light, iron boxes for specie, jewelry, and valuables, are securely attached as fixtures in each coach. The material fact, however, on this point is, that this line of route is seldom visited by robbers, owing to the more peaceful, permanent, and dense character of the population, and the consequent exposure to detection. General Santa Ana has, moreover, made a decree that the inhabitants of each district shall be responsible for the damages by such depredations.

Much more might be said in relation to this route, but this memorial has already become too long. Reiterating our former assertion, that we only ask the opportunity of placing ourselves honorably before Congress, on our own integrity, we hope that our enterprise may receive such official sanction from the Post Office Department as may be most compatible with the interests of the government and the benefit of the community.

With great respect, your obedient servant,

ROBERT G. RANKIN,
President M. O. M. & I. Co.

Hon. JAMES CAMPBELL,
Postmaster General.

APPENDIX A.

I hereby certify that I am intimately acquainted with the road between Vera Cruz and Puebla, and thence to Acapulco.

Having been engaged in mercantile business at Puebla for the last seven years, I am intimately acquainted with every mile of this road, having, from the nature of my business, been compelled often to travel over the whole route, and am therefore free to say that the whole distance can be travelled in stage-coaches without any impediment—this road being free from robbers—and will require only an expenditure of from $25,000 to $30,000, to make it equal to any stage route in the United States; and at this time, without the expenditure of even a single dollar, the whole distance can be travelled in stage-coaches, with the exception of about thirteen leagues, with the utmost facility and expedition. The mail is now taken from Vera Cruz to Acapulco in sixty hours, which time will be shortly reduced to fifty hours; and this distance can be regularly travelled with the mail coaches in that space of time the whole year round.

J. BLUMENKRON.

CITY OF NEW YORK, *November* 22, 1853.

APPENDIX B.

Extracts from letters received from Colonel Ramsey, in Mexico, of the dates following.

"AUGUST 29, 1853.

"I have received a letter from Mr. Markoe, an agent at Vera Cruz, dated August 22, in which he says: 'The Texas left this morning at 8 o'clock a. m. The express arrived last night at 8. It left Acapulco on the 17th at 4 p. m.' Mr. Tyler writes me: 'The riders have done nobly in getting through in the time they did, considering the state of the roads, (in the height of the rainy season.)' Mr. Denman, at Acapulco, writes me from Acapulco, August 23: 'Your express which left Vera Cruz on the 17th instant at 4 p. m., arrived here on the 22d at 4½ a. m.' "

"SEPTEMBER 15, 1853.

"I only returned last evening from a trip I have been making over some distance of our route. The express mail is not working to my entire satisfaction, as too much time (80 hours) is too long, and I am anxious to improve this important service."

"By the time that the rains are over, all our animals will be in prime condition—say by the 1st November—and then our agents assure me they can easily make the distance under 60 hours. This season has been unprecedented for heavy rains and bad roads. We have now passed through the worst of it, making the experiment under every possible disadvantage, and proving that we can always run from port to port in 80 hours at the farthest."

"I have a letter from Señor Gernez, the Secretary of State of Guerrero, dated the 7th instant, in which he says: 'The courier left Acapulco on the 4th instant, at 4 p. m., and arrived here, (Tixtla,) in this city, on the 5th, at 2 o'clock p. m.' Now, by looking at the distance, you will perceive that it is over the worst part of the road, and more than one hundred* miles, at the very worst season of the year."

"OCTOBER 3, 1853.

"I have been informed by the agent of the Pacific Mail Steamship Company at Acapulco that the steamers will not hereafter touch at that port. If this be the fact, it will be grave matter for the consid-

* The distance has since been reduced.

eration of our company. In that event, we will be cut off from receiving or forwarding any California mails until we establish a connexion of our own.''

"The careful examination I have directed to be made recently of the whole length of our route, has dispelled many of the obstacles and difficultias which we had supposed would have to be encountered. I always supposed that, as we became more familiar with the route, and with the country on both sides of it, difficulties would vanish.

"Our express mail has not only demonstrated the time in which we can run over the route, but also the obstacles in the very worst season of the very worst year.''

"My last reports received of the time of the couriers from Vera Cruz, on the 17th September, 4 p. m., were as follows: Arrived at Puebla 4 p. m. on the 18th; arrived at Mitapec 11 a. m. on the 19th; arrived at Draper 3½ p. m. on the 19th; arrived at Papagallos river 10 a. m. of the 20th; arrived at Acapulco at 6 p. m. of the 20th—the whole time three days and two hours. At least four hours were lost by the courier going through Chilpanzingo, which was out of the way.''

"OCTOBER 15, 1853.

"Since writing the above, I have thought it best to finish the subject of the gold-placers on the Mescala river. The existence of these mines have long been known. You will find them mentioned in my notes on this valley, under the article on 'Mines;' but recently gold has been found in such abundance as to cause a sensation; people rush in crowds.

"Since then other more extensive placers have been discovered on the Papagallos river, in the line of our route. These have created a still greater sensation, as you will see by the papers. My notes on the mines are almost incredible; but it is gratifying to find every day new confirmation of all that I described of the astonishing mineral wealth of that country.

"If I can leave the city in order to attend more closely to this express line, I could soon convince you that eighty hours is slow travelling. The last reports I sent you show an improvement on this, by reducing the time to seventy hours. My orders will now, I trust, be obeyed, as it is pretty evident I will take no excuses. I have now ordered the mail to be carried in sixty hours, which is only a beginning. If my orders are carried out, in six weeks time *I will have it done in forty-eight hours, which will be at about seven miles per hour. This is no great feat in such a country, in such a climate, and on such roads.* Were the horses now in the proper condition, which they would be, had they been properly fed and attended to, I could now perform it in forty-eight hours. You remark, 'the route being feasible for an express mail under all the difficulties incident to such an enterprise, why not feasible for heavy mails and passengers?' To this let me answer that the route, beyond all question, is feasible for heavy mails, as much so as for light mails; we will gain vastly in time as soon as we can put on our stages.

"You must have been in mind that between Rincon and the crossing of the Papagallos there are no mountains; and, to make the road practicable for stages, it only requires some widening at the most trifling expense. Our Concord wagons will suit admirably for this purpose.

"I am ashamed of our contract to carry the California mail to New Orleans in sixteen days, when I know we can carry it even to New York in a less number of days. It has actually placed us in a false position, from which we ought to relieve ourselves by a practical demonstration.

"I regret extremely that the steamers have not joined us at the ends of our route, so that we could demonstrate the few hours in which we can make the distance across Mexico. All that I may report to you—all the certificates of speed—will not satisfy the public; they must have the letters and news from California. It is your affair to require them to make the connexion."

Acapulco, *September* 23, 1853.

Dear Sir: I have to acknowledge the receipt of yours of the 16th September. In reference to your metallic-boat, it is in good order, excepting that the air-chambers have been cut open for the purpose of stowing baggage.

It is with much gratification that I received correspondence from New Orleans in six days, by your last mail, which arrived here on the 20th instant at 7¼ o'clock p. m.; and I am now satisfied that, at present, this route presents facilities for the most rapid mail communication between California and the United States.

Yours, truly,

S. TYLER, *Agent.*

Albert C. Ramsey, Esq.,
Vice President and Agent, Mexico.

Office P. M. S. S. Co.,
Acapulco, September 21, 1853.

Dear Sir: Your mail was received last night at 6 o'clock, bringing dates from New Orleans to the 14th inst., which is very satisfactory, being as yet, I think, the quickest time from the United States.

The down boat from San Francisco I have advised you will not touch, for which I am very sorry; but your mail matter will receive quick despatch for San Francisco.

Yours, truly,

S. TYLER, *Agent.*

Albert C. Ramsey, Esq., *Mexico.*

[From the Universal, September 19, 1853.]

Improvements in the State of Puebla.

The Eco del Comercio of Vera Cruz, in its number of the 14th inst., (September, 1853,) has the following paragraphs:

"The Prefectura of Matamoras, in the State of Puebla, have under their charge the repairing of the road which connects that State with the State of Guerrero, and the work has been under the direction of Senor José Maria Pavon since last January, with 70 presidential soldiers, afterwards increased 80, provided with plenty of tools, rations, and clothes from the municipal funds. In the first three months of that year, 15,000 yards of road were opened near Mitapec to the State line of Guerrero; and to the last dates, the 31st July last, 3,563 yards were repaired near Chietta; and near Tepeojiema, (S. Juan Espanthan,) 8,529 yards.

Order of the Mexican government to facilitate our mails.—General direction of mails.

MEXICO, *July* 18, 1853.

In a supreme order of the 6th inst., which I received on the 16th, his excellency the Minister of Hacienda (Treasury) writes to me as follows:

"His excellency the President is informed, by your official despatch No. 95, dated the 22d of June last, of the improvements introduced by Mr. Albert C. Ramsey in the line of steamers between Acapulco and San Francisco, in California, and between New Orleans and Vera Cruz, and in that of mails from that port to Acapulco, whose days of arrival and departure are stated in the copy which accompanies yours; and you ask to be authorized to publish the same. His excellency has been pleased to accord this permission, which I communicate to you in answer for that purpose. To the same effect, their excellencies the governors of the States of Vera Cruz, Puebla, Mexico, and Guerrero have been written to, to place no obstacle in the way of the fixing the posts of Senor Ramsey, but, on the contrary, to afford every facility in placing these very useful establishments."

I have the honor of transmitting this to you for your information, and in answer to your communications of the 16th June last and the 12th inst., assuring you of my consideration and particular esteem.

God and liberty.

P. M. ANAYA.

To Mr. ALBERT C. RAMSEY.

General direction of mails.

MEXICO, *July* 18, 1853.

By virtue of the contract (by supreme approbation) made with Don Alberte C. Ramsey, with this general direction, to transport through the territory of the republic the mails coming from foreign places, and going also to foreign ports, by means of the ocean line of steamers between Vera Cruz and New Orleans, and between Acapulco and San Francisco, in California, the said Mr. Ramsey has arranged the trips of the said mails in the following manner:

Line of steamers between Vera Cruz and New Orleans.—Leave New Orleans every month the 1st, 14th, and 25th; arrive at Vera Cruz the 4th, 17th, and 28th. Leave Vera Cruz the 1st, 8th, and 22d; arrive at New Orleans the 4th, 11th, and 25th.

Line of steamers between Acapulco and San Francisco, connecting with the express from Vera Cruz to Acapulco.—Leave Vera Cruz every month the 4th and 17th; arrive at Acapulco the 9th and 22d. Leave Acapulco the 9th and 22d; arrive at San Francisco the 17th and 30th. Leave San Francisco the 8th and 24th; arrive at Acapulco the 16th and 1st. Leave Acapulco the 16th and 1st; arrive at Vera Cruz the 21st and 6th.

All of which is, by supreme order, published for information.

P. M. ANAYA.

NEW YORK, *November* 28, 1854.

SIR: The undersigned would respectfully call your attention to their contract of the 3d of March, 1852, with the department, for the transportation of the United States mails between Vera Cruz, in Mexico, and Acapulco, San Diego, Monterey, and San Francisco. By this contract it was stipulated and intended to transport the mails semi-monthly between New Orleans and San Francisco in sixteen days, (consecutively,) and surety for a large amount was given for the faithful performance of the service. By the terms of this contract it was subject to the approval of Congress, and also to an appropriation by the same.

The undersigned immediately prepared to perform the service in order to satisfy the requirements of the department, and also to save their surety harmless from their heavy obligation. Steamers were provided for the service on the Pacific ocean, and one of the undersigned proceeded to Mexico to take charge of the line between Vera Cruz and Acapulco. Horses, mules, harness, stages, wagons, and other materiel, were rapidly collected to furnish all that was required for the 384 miles of land conveyance across Mexico. At the same time a small letter mail was established, which commenced operations in July of the same year. By this method it was designed to transmit, rapidly, intelligence between the Atlantic and Pacific cities of the Union until the stages and other materiel, were properly placed on the line. Under this temporary arrangement, newspapers and letters were carried between California and New Orleans in fourteen, thirteen, and twelve-and-a-half days. Had the arrangement been completed for connecting with the steamers at Vera Cruz and Acapulco, in no instance would the time have exceeded thirteen days, as the distance by land across Mexico, from sea to sea, was performed with great ease and security in less than three days. Frequent experiments were made on parts of the Mexican road to test the time required for the transportation of the mails when the stages were placed on the route, and it was found that as soon as the mails were transported in the vehicles prepared for that purpose, the time would not exceed forty-eight consecutive hours between Vera Cruz and Acapulco.

It was the intention of the undersigned to have commenced with the mail stages in the month of December, as they were all ready prepared and on the ground for that purpose. The expenses incurred under the contract at that time, amounted to the sum of ninety-eight thousand dollars, ($98,000,) of which $56,000 have been paid, and the balance remains unliquidated. But the department having at this time expressed, in an annual report to Congress, a disapprobation of the contract on the ground of the impolicy of conditional contracts, the undersigned ceased their operations, and, consequently, have sustained serious damages from the action of the department. It is to be regretted that the department should have interposed to break up this enterprise, which, by the terms of the contract, was to be exclusively in the power of Congress. It is also to be regretted that this route, the shortest and best for the rapid transmission of the mails, should thus remain unoccupied at the present time. The undersigned are still ready and willing to perform the service in the time and mode specified, and would further suggest that if they were not required to touch at Monterey and San Diego, they would further stipulate to carry the mails, at all times, so as to make each trip between San Francisco and New Orleans in less than thirteen days. By the other routes the time now required is some nine or ten days more. Thus an important saving of time would be effected, and a corresponding benefit to the public.

Very respectfully, your obedient servants,
ALBERT C. RAMSEY.
EDWARD H. CARMICK.

Hon. JAMES CAMPBELL,
Postmaster General.

POST OFFICE DEPARTMENT,
November 30, 1854.

GENTLEMEN: Your letter of the 28th instant has been received. The conditional contract for service between San Francisco and Vera Cruz, to which you refer, was executed on the 3d of March, 1853, just before I came into office. My attention was called to the subject of Mr. Rankin's letter of the 16th of June, 1853. In my letter of the 9th July following, I gave my views at length in regard to this contract; and if sums of money were expended by you after that time, it was done with a full knowledge of my views, which remain unchanged.

I am, respectfully, your obedient servant,

JAMES CAMPBELL,
Postmaster General.

Messrs. RAMSEY & CARMICK,
New York, N. Y.

NEW YORK, *December* 20, 1854.

SIR: Your letter of the 30th ultimo was duly received. In referring to the contract between the department and ourselves, you say that, on the 9th of July, 1853, you made known your disapproval of the contract in a communication in answer to a letter from R. G. Rankin; and if we have expended money after that time, on account of the contract, we have done so with a full knowledge of your views.

We were not informed, by your letter of the 9th of July, that you had any intention of annulling our contract. We had completed all our arrangements for stocking the road across Mexico prior to the receipt of your letter; and, on account of the same, have expended the sum of ninety-eight thousand dollars, ($98,000;) and our surety for the faithful performance of the contract had been given, and we were bound to be ready to carry the mails.

Your letter certainly did not annul the contract; for then our sureties would have been released from all responsibility on our account, and we absolved from all reproach for the failure of the enterprise. On the contrary, the department still considered the contract binding upon us, as is apparent from the subsequent correspondence with Messrs. Harris & Morgan. The steamers belonging to these gentlemen were carrying the United States mail between that city and Vera Cruz. They had addressed you on the subject of a change in the days of departure from each port, so as to connect, by means of our line across Mexico, with the Panama steamers, at Acapulco, running to San Francisco; and thus supplying additional facilities for a more rapid and frequent transmission of intelligence to and from California. The advantage of this arrangement would have been immense to the Atlantic and Pacific cities, without any inconvenience to the department, and moreover without one dollar expense to it; of course, this arrangement was intended to continue only until the appropriation should be made under our contract, when steamers were to be placed on the line between Acapulco and San Francisco.

The wishes of Messrs. Harris & Morgan, as well as those of the Pacific Mail Steamship Company, desiring this temporary change in the schedule time between New Orleans and Vera Cruz, were fully communicated in writing to the department. But in your letter to Messrs. Harris & Morgan of the 3d of November, 1853, you refused to accede to this request; predicating your refusal on our contract made with your predecessor, Mr. Hubbard, for the transmission of a semi-monthly California mail, in which it was not contemplated that the mails sent from New Orleans, via Vera Cruz and Acapulco, should go forward to California by the Panama steamers, but by another line running only between Acapulco and San Francisco; and which contract was awaiting the sanction of Congress. You add: "No such sanction has yet been given by Congress; but apart from this, and without troubling you with my views on the subject, it is simply necessary for me to say, that there can be no recognition by the department of any arrangement by which the additional semi-monthly mail, clearly contemplated by the then Postmaster General, can be dispensed with." In this there is a positive recognition of our contract or arrangement with Mr. Hubbard as still existing, which the department would not "dispense with," although it would, while our appropriation was pending, have shortened the time some ten days to and from California by connecting with the Panama steamers touching at Acapulco.

When the annual report of the Post Office Department, in December, 1853, was transmitted to Congress, we were led to believe, for the first time, that you had decided virtually to annul our contract, as the estimate for an appropriation under the contract was not sent in by you, but another route for a semi-monthly mail was recommended. You will thus perceive we were not apprized of the intentions of the department until the close of the year 1853, when all our expenses had been incurred, and when, in consequence of the official report, our operations ceased.

In conclusion, the department, by its action, having virtually annulled the contract, and having assumed to do that which, by the terms of the contract, was left to Congress, we therefore deem ourselves grievously damaged, and have more than an equitable claim for redress.

Very respectfully, your obedient servants,

ALBERT C. RAMSEY.
E. H. CARMICK.

Hon. JAMES CAMPBELL,
Postmaster General.

www.ingramcontent.com/pod-product-compliance
Lightning Source LLC
LaVergne TN
LVHW011135110826
845150LV00008B/2368

* 9 7 8 1 4 1 8 1 9 4 3 4 5 *